**PRIZES!**

 **STOP**

 **$50 GIFT CARD**

# Think YOU can win our JOKE CONTEST?!?!

The Don't Laugh Challenge is having a **CONTEST** to see who is the **MOST HILARIOUS** boy or girl in the USA.

Please have your parents email us your best \*\*original\*\* joke and you could win a $50 gift card to Amazon.

Here are the rules:

1. It must be funny. Please do not give us jokes that aren't funny. We get enough of those from our joke writers

2. It must be original. We have computers and we know how to use them.

3. No help from the parents. Plus, they aren't even that funny anyway!!

## Email your best joke to:

 **Bacchuspublish@gmail.com**

Winners will be announced via email.

Bacchus Publishing House

# The Don't Laugh™ Challenge
## Instructions:

- Stand in front of your opponent face-to-face.

- Take turns reading jokes to each other.

- First person to make the opponent laugh, wins a point!

- First person to 3 points wins & is crowned The Don't Laugh MASTER.

# Game on!

# EASTER JOKES

When the chicks were being put to bed, Mama Hen said, "I don't want to hear a PEEP!"

Easter Eggs are the best audience for comedy. They always CRACK UP!

The Bunnies were so close at the end of the race. They were a HARE apart!

Painting all those eggs is hard work, that's why the Easter Bunny has to DYE-it!

What is the Easter Bunny's
favorite reggae song?

"Don't worry, Be Hoppy."

Easter Egg candy is really shy. They
never want to come out of their SHELL.

Chocolate Bunnies love Hip Hop, and you
can tell because they jump a lot and come
in WRAPPERS!

Which Easter Egg won the contest for
"Best Decorated"?

None, they were all tie-dyed!

Why was the floor wrong to laugh at the broken egg?

Because the yolk was on them!

Did you hear about the close race between the two rabbits?

It was won by a hare!

What does the Easter Bunny plant in his garden, but never grows?

Jelly Beans!

What do a bald man, and a zoo with no rabbits have in common?

They're both HARE-less!

What is the Easter Bunny's
favorite game?
Hide and go seek!

What is the fastest kind of egg?
A runny egg!

What's an Egg's least favorite day?
Fry-day!

What do you call the illegal
cooking of eggs?
Poaching!

When I meet the Easter Bunny,
I will be so EGGS-cited!

Why do chickens work?
They have to make the big buck buck buuucks!

Why did the Easter Bunny walk
gently around the eggs?
He was walking on eggshells!

What did the Easter eggs do on
April Fool's day?
They hatched a hilarious plan...

What do you call a really funny
Easter Egg?
A Comedi-HEN!

Where do Easter Eggs
go on vacation?
Easter Island!

What's a great name for
my Easter egg?
Mi-shell!

What did the Egg say when
its bicycle crashed?
"I'll just have to roll with it!"

What did the Chick say when
the ceiling was too low?
"Duck!"

What did the Egg say on the
first day of school?
"Let's get cracking!"

How did the Bunny fix her trampoline?
She replaced the spring!

What does a bunny use to style its fur?
Hare spray!

What do you call it when flowers kiss?
Tulips!

How do you dry a wet Rabbit?
Use a hare-dryer!

What season gives Bunnies
their bounce?
SPRING!

What does a Rabbit say when
it laughs really hard?
"That's BUNNY!"

To paint the perfect Egg,
you must be EGG-sact!

Why did the rooster cross the road?
He wanted to impress the chicks!

Knock Knock.
Who's there?
Cadbury.
Cadbury, who?
No, you Cadbury my Easter Candy!

Whenever someone talks about the
Easter Bunny, I'm ALL EARS!

Egg races are always a SCRAMBLE to the finish line!

I told my Easter jokes to the Lambs, they said all of them were BAAAAAAD!

No wonder rabbits jump around so much. If I were full of chocolate eggs, I'd be HOPPED up too!

After we painted the eggs, the Easter Bunny said mine were EGGS-cellent!

I call Easter the lazy Halloween because we still get candy, and no one has to dress up!

Egg Spoon Races are a great place to practice concentration under EGGS-treme circumstances.

Easter Eggs never think about anyone else. They're all so SHELL-fish!

What does an Easter Chick say when it hatches?
"SHELL-O!"

Every Chick loves its shell,
that is until they BREAK-UP!


What did the Bunny say on the
first day of school?
"Let's hop to it!"


What is a Trampoline's favorite season?
Spring!


What is the Easter Bunny's
favorite song?
"If You're Hoppy and You Know It!"

Easter Eggs are best raw...
Ha ha, I'm just YOLKING!

Why was the baby chicken so popular?
Because she was a cool chick.

How did the Easter Bunny stay
in such good shape?
A good diet, and plenty of eggs-cercise!

Who is the highest ranking
egg in the Army?
The most highly decorated!

Why do some people wear
camouflage on Easter?
Because they're on the hunt!

What did the tall Easter Bunny
say when people teased him?
"Long hare, don't care!"

What's a Hen's favorite snack?
A chickpea!

What's a Chicken's favorite composer?
Bach!

What do you do when an
Easter Egg hatches?
SHELL-ebrate!

Why did the Easter Egg not
want to get painted?
It was a free-range spirit...

What do you call an Easter Egg
you throw too far?
Foul ball!

With whom did the Easter Egg fall
in love with?
The Egg NEST door.

# Why were the Easter Eggs so nice?
They were made of complementary colors!

# What do you call it when an Easter Bunny paints a picture of himself?
A paw-trait!

# What's a normal Doctors visit for an Easter Egg?
An EGGS-amination!

# What did the Conductor say when the Bunny got on the train?
"Hop on board!"

What sound does a baby
Marshmallow make?
"Peep peep!"

What do you call a bunny with no fur?
Hare-less.

This year's Egg Painting Show
was to DYE for!

All this Candy, Eggs, and Bunnies!
Whoever came up with this is a
BASKET case!

Knock Knock.
Who's there?
Choco-late.
Choco-late, who?
No, you're right on time!


Why was everyone laughing at the
Easter Egg?
It kept cracking jokes!


The Easter Bunny needs
chocolate to EGG-sist!


It's a lot of work for a Chick to hatch all
by themselves, they have to be
SHELL-f motivated!

## What is the Easter Bunny's favorite kind of race?

The Three L-EGG-ed Race!

## What type of Easter candy sleeps the best at night?

Cadbury Dream Eggs.

## What is a Bunny's favorite Olympic event?

High jump!

## What did the Lamb say when it smelled a skunk?

Ewe!

What did the Easter Bunny laugh at
all the Ducks' jokes?

He quacked him up!

What did the Easter Bunny get
his wife on their anniversary?

A necklace made out of 24-Carrot gold!

What is the Easter Bunny's favorite
art medium?

Pastels!

What do you call two Easter Eggs
that are best friends?

Yolked!

What do you call an Easter Egg
with no sense of humor?

Hard-shelled.

What do you call a Chicken
that's not married?

A BACH-elor!

What do you call two fighting
Easter Eggs?

Foul play!

What do you call it when an
Easter Egg misses its mom?

Nest-olgia!

What do you call an Easter Egg
with a great attitude?

Sunny side up!

What did the Paint say to the
Easter Egg?

"I've got you covered."

Where did the Easter Bunny look to
find out more about Easter Eggs?

In the HEN-cyclopedia!

Where does an Easter Egg go to learn?

EGG-lementary school!

How do you get a chick out of a spaceship?
Open the hatch!

Why do pigs make such good actors?
They're always HAM-ming it up!

What was the Easter Egg's favorite type of music?
Rock and Roll!

Where do Bunnies get their water?
From a spring!

What did the Marshmallow say to her children when she hid the Easter Eggs?

"No PEEP-ing!"

What do you call a Bunny with orange fur?

A carrot top!

What do Bunnies give each other for Christmas?

Gift baskets.

Why couldn't the Lamb ask out the other Lamb on a date?

He was too sheepish!

What did the Mom say when the jelly bean kept yelling in public?
"You're BEAN too loud!"

# HAPPY EASTER!

# FUNNY JOKES

## Why did the Bowler get fired from his job?

He was on his last strike!

## What do you call a dog that plays football?

A Labrador RECEIVER!

## Why did the Dolphin want to study Philosophy?

He was trying to find the porpoise of life.

## Why did everyone love going to Casper's dinner parties?

Because he was always the ghostess, with the mostess!

What is a fashion designer's favorite
kind of chips?
Ruffles.

Why can't icebergs tell jokes?
They'll crack up!

Why did the cookie lose
the spelling bee?
It crumbled under pressure.

What did the baker say to the bread?
Let's rise early!

Why was the knife being so
nice to the toast?

To butter him up!

What did the parmesan say
to the cheddar?

"Good things come to those who grate."

Why don't people like spicy peppers?

Because they get jalapeño business.

What is a can of soda's favorite
type of music?

POP!

What is Rapunzel's favorite
piece of advice?
"Let your hair down."

What happened to the baseball glove
that accidentally went
through the spin cycle?
He was all washed up!

Why should you bring Merida to a
scary movie?
Because she's BRAVE!

What do Unicorns say to warn each
other about roughhousing?
"It's all fun and games until someone loses an eye."

What do you call a boat full of teeth?
A Tooth Ferry!

What is a Pig's favorite ice cream?
HOG-en-Dazs!

What happened when they ran out
of Hot Fudge for my Sundae?
Ice creamed!

What do you call a Sasquatch who likes
to make things out of clay?
A Hairy Potter!

# Why was the mirror sent to his room?
To reflect on his decisions.

# What does a tree say to his crush?
"Wood you be my valenpine?"

# How did the two gymnasts divide their winnings?
They SPLIT it!

# Where did the Lawyer go to play basketball?
The court.

## What kind of dog makes the best artwork?

A Labra-DOODLE!

## Why didn't the Pepperoni laugh at the Pizza's joke?

It was really cheesy!

## What did the Cat say when it got trapped?

"Get MEOW-ta here!"

## Why did the bicycle take a nap?

He was two tired!

What do you call it when
celebrities fight?
Star Wars!

What did the hand say to the mitten he
had a crush on?
"I think I'm in GLOVE!"

Why did the Cat love
brushing his teeth?
He gets to use MOUSE wash!

Why did the Dog always get in fights?
He was a Boxer!

# How did the golf ball ace his test?
He answered the questions to a tee!

# What did the fork say to the spoon before he left?
"Don't FORK-et me!"

# What did a Raisin say to his neighbor?
"It's grape to see you!"

# What did the milk say to the coffee?
"Lighten up!"

Which fish went to Hollywood and became famous?

A Starfish.

What animal has a million questions and never leaves you alone?

A Badger.

Why are Geese bad drivers?

They honk at everyone!

Why do birds avoid the airport?

They hate long flights.

# What did the tree say to the dog?
"You're barking up the wrong tree!"

# What's a dog's favorite meal?
PAWsta!

# What did the cowboy say to the artist?
"Draw!"

# If a King and a Queen are a pair when sitting on a throne, what are they when sitting on a toilet?
A Royal Flush.

# Why do park benches always yawn?
They're so board.

# Why couldn't the arrow make any friends?
It was always pointing at people!

# Why did the maid plant trees inside the house?
She was asked to Spruce up!

# How much does lightning weigh?
Not much. It's light.

Why did the mirror feel down
on his luck?

He was broke.

What game do ants like to play?

Follow the leader.

What's a Librarian's favorite past time?

Shushing.

What kind of hairstyle does
a horseback rider like?

A ponytail.

# What is a Cereal's favorite sport?
BOWL-ing!

# What did the Hawk say to the funny Owl?
"You're a hoot!"

# What is a Golfer's favorite home goods store?
The Putt-ery Barn.

# Why couldn't the Zombie collect life insurance?
Because he was undead!

# Why was the Cow mean to his friends?

He was in a bad MOO-d!

# Which planet is the best musician?

NepTUNE.

# Why did one iceberg ignore the other iceberg?

It was giving it the cold shoulder.

# Which bugs are best at espionage?

SPYders.

# Who hides inside an egg?
Someone who's a little chicken.

# Why are fish easy to weigh?
They have their own scales!

# What kind of cow can you bring in a bank?
A cash cow!

# How does a horse hold a job?
They are NEIGH-ver late.

What is a rabbit's favorite
type of dance?

A sock hop.

What do you call it when you spin your
meal around on the tip of your finger?

A fidget dinner!

What does the sign on the front
of a beehive say?

"Open for buzziness."

Why didn't the fan win the race?

He blew it.

Why couldn't the squirrel
make a decision?

He was always on the fence.

What does the Hammer say at the
end of the work day?

"Nailed it!"

How could the flute
remember everything?

It was actually a recorder!

What did the Lamp say to his wife?

"Honey, you're absolutely glowing!"

What is a Writer's favorite
place to sleep?
An alpha-bed.

Why did the cloud love the snowflakes?
They're down to Earth!

Why was the saxophone working out?
To be as fit as the fiddle!

Why is the Hulk growing a garden?
He has a green thumb.

Why was the jar of jelly late to work?
There was a bit of a jam.

What did one nut say to the other when they were playing tag?
"I'm gonna cashew!"

Was it hard for the baker to cut through the dessert?
No, no! It was a piece of cake!

What's wrong with the jokes cheddar makes?
They're too cheesy.

Why could no one read
the Hen's writing?

It was chicken scratch.

How do horses gain extra time?

They stall!

How did the crab pay for its ice cream?

A Sand dollar.

How did everyone know the
horse was rich?

He could always pony up!

# What's a Firefly's favorite dance?
## The Glitterbug.

# Who's the most popular animal Pop Star?
## Justin Beaver!

# What do an Alien and Mickey Mouse have in common?
## They both love Pluto!

# What is the Golfer's favorite cut of meat?
## Tee-bone!

Why couldn't Humpty Dumpty
go out to dinner?

He was broke!

What do you call an invisible bear?

BEAR-ly there!

How does an Art Collector
like his steak?

Rare.

What type of birds works
construction?

Cranes!

How do you know when a
snake is upset?

It gets HISS-terical.

What is a cow's favorite type of snow?

Cornflakes!

Why is it so hard to do business
with bulls?

Because they like to charge a lot!

Why didn't the Teacher cover the
chapter on porcupines?

She didn't want to touch on that topic!

Why was the white crayon
self-conscious?

Because he paled in comparison.

How did the diaper say he was feeling?

"Just a little down in the dumps."

What happened to the
World Sugar Association?

It eventually dissolved.

Why can't you trust pants?

They always pocket your money.

# What happened when the apples got married?

They lived Apple-y ever after!

# Why can't you trust a clock with your secrets?

Because time will tell!

# Why didn't the chalkboard take a bath?

It was a clean slate.

# Why was the shoe so nice to everyone?

It had a good sole.

What do you call a cow taking a nap?
Ground beef.

When did the secretive grape
spill everything?
When it went to the press.

Have you tried the new
jam-and-jelly buffet?
They have a lovely spread.

Why did the Cat want everyone to
try her brownies?
Because she made them from scratch!

Who always gets ripped off
from the store?

The price tag!

How did the Sun get so many planets?

It gave them a warm welcome!

What happens when a sausage has
a bad dream?

Your wurst nightmare!

Why did the Tortilla Chip go to
the pool party?

It wanted to take a dip!

Why do teachers always put
the skeleton in the corner?
They are bad to the bone.

Why couldn't the band go on a cruise?
You shouldn't rock the boat!

What did the Astronomy teacher
say to his students?
"Aim for the stars!"

How do Pegasuses fly?
On a wing and a prayer.

How does a train eat its food?
It chew-chews.

What happens to an orange if
it gets a sunburn?
It starts to peel.

Can one tropical bird change
a light bulb?
No, but Toucan!

Why don't eggs go to the tanning salon?
They don't want to get fried!

What do bunnies like to do at the mall?

Shop 'til they hop!

Why didn't the little girl like
wearing diamonds?

She was too cool for jewels.

What is a Fairy's favorite
type of haircut?

A pixie cut.

Why was the cardboard so
bad at poker?

It was a folder!

What do you call a broken watch?
A waste of time!

What do you call shoes
that are undercover?
Sneakers.

What happened when the wave
graduated from High school?
He swelled with pride!

What kind of dog would be friends
with a crab?
A Doberman PINCH-er.

# How did the Shoes get kicked out of the bar?

They were given the boot.

# Why did the Jam want to become a Journalist?

It wanted to spread the news!

# Why was the Shoelace late for his appointment?

He got tied up!

# Why did the Pencil give up drawing?

He didn't see the point.

What kind of crustacean
likes to keep to itself?
A Hermit Crab.

What is a Vampire's least favorite meat?
Steak.

Why couldn't the Alligator
reach his friends?
He couldn't croco-DIAL the phone!

What color are the Cat's teeth?
Purr-ly white!

# Why couldn't the Boy stop laughing at the Doctor's office?

The Doctor had him in stitches!

# What is a Golfer's favorite drink?

Tea!

# Why did no one take the Duck seriously?

It was always quacking jokes!

# Why did the Chicken cross the playground?

To get to the other slide.

Why didn't the dim light bulb do well in school?

He wasn't very bright.

What happens when you take tea away from a young toad?

He becomes oad.

Why did the Surfer swim back to shore?

He couldn't wave good-bye.

What happens when you use spot remover on a leopard?

Nothing. A leopard can't change its spot and neither can you!

A student pilot was on her first
training flight with her flight instructor.
"How do you fly this thing?",
She asked him. The instructor replied,
"I just wing it."

Why can't Monday lift Saturday?
It's a weak day.

What did the string say to the scissors
when they were sitting in traffic?
"Don't cut me off!"

Why was the politician out of breath?
He was running for office.

How did the cell phone propose?

He gave her a ring.

Why couldn't the broom stay awake?

He was sweepy.

Why did the wife kick the fisherman
out of the house?

He was being crabby.

Why is Princess Aurora
always late for class?

Because she's trying to catch up
on her beauty sleep.

Why do electrical outlets give such good advice?

They're very grounded.

What did the roller coaster say when the amusement park closed?

"It's just not fair!"

What kind of sea creature never loses power?

An Electric Eel.

What do you call a cat in a police officer's uniform?

A Paw Enforcement Officer.

Why didn't the Hammerhead
Shark feel well?
His head was pounding.

For which crimes are cats
most known?
Kitty littering.

What did one toad say to the other?
"Warts up?!"

How does a spider know where
to go to find flies?
He searches the web!

# Why didn't the window have anything to do?

His schedule was all clear.

# Why did the Army Recruit not understand his Commander's instructions?

He was being too GENERAL!

# What is Ariel's favorite kind of story?

She prefers a good fish-out-of-water tale!

# What kind of pig doesn't say oink?

A Guinea Pig.

What do you get when you cross
a bee with an eagle?

A Beagle.

Why was the lamb acting so shy?

He was feeling sheepish.

Which animal is the
greatest of all time?

A G.O.A.T.

What is a Bumblebee's favorite
line from Shakespeare?

"To bee or not to bee that
is the question."

# What do you call a substitute musician?

Band-Aid.

# Why did the Opera Singer's pants fall down?

He was belting it out.

# What animal is always laid-back?

A ChinCHILLa.

Made in the USA
Lexington, KY
21 March 2019

# The Don't Laugh Challenge™

## Easter Edition
## · Volume 2 ·